DODD, MEAD WONDERS BOOKS include WONDERS OF:

ALLIGATORS AND CROCODILES. Blassingame
ANIMAL NURSERIES. Berrill
BARNACLES. Ross and Emerson
BAT WORLD. Lavine
BEYOND THE SOLAR SYSTEM. Feravolo
BISON WORLD. Lavine and Scuro
CACTUS WORLD. Lavine
CAMELS. Lavine
CARIBOU. Rearden
CORALS AND CORAL REEFS. Jacobson and Franz
CROWS. Blassingame
DINOSAUR WORLD. Matthews
DONKEYS. Lavine and Scuro
EAGLE WORLD. Lavine
FLY WORLD. Lavine
FROGS AND TOADS. Blassingame
GEESE AND SWANS. Fegely
GEMS. Pearl
GRAVITY. Feravolo
HAWK WORLD. Lavine
HERBS. Lavine
HUMMINGBIRDS. Simon
JELLYFISH. Jacobson and Franz
KELP FOREST. Brown
LLAMAS. Perry
LIONS. Schaller
MARSUPIALS. Lavine
MEASUREMENT. Lieberg

MONKEY WORLD. Berrill
MOSQUITO WORLD. Ault
OWL WORLD. Lavine
PELICAN WORLD. Cook and Schreiber
PRAIRIE DOGS. Chace
PRONGHORN. Chace
RACCOONS. Blassingame
ROCKS AND MINERALS. Pearl
SEA GULLS. Schreiber
SEA HORSES. Brown
SEALS AND SEA LIONS. Brown
SPIDER WORLD. Lavine
SPONGES. Jacobson and Pang
STARFISH. Jacobson and Emerson
STORKS. Kahl
TERNS. Schreiber
TERRARIUMS. Lavine
TREE WORLD. Cosgrove
TURTLE WORLD. Blassingame
WILD DUCKS. Fegely
WOODS AND DESERT AT NIGHT. Berrill
WORLD OF THE ALBATROSS. Fisher
WORLD OF BEARS. Bailey
WORLD OF HORSES. Lavine and Casey
WORLD OF SHELLS. Jacobson and Emerson
WORLD OF WOLVES. Berrill
YOUR SENSES. Cosgrove

# Wonders of CROWS

Wyatt Blassingame

*Illustrated with photographs and line drawings*

DODD, MEAD & COMPANY · NEW YORK

ILLUSTRATION CREDITS
Leona Anderson, 8, 76; Cliff Bickford, 58, 86; Wyatt Blassingame, 69, 89, 91; A. D. Cruickshank, 81; Kathi Diamant, 19, 20, 70; Whitney J. Dough, Methodist Hour, Inc., 10, 73, 74; Florida Audubon Society, 55; Florida Game & Fresh Water Fish Commission, 2 (by Lovett Williams), 13 (by Lovett Williams), 23 (by Lovett Williams), 38 (by Wallace Hughes), 49 (by Lovett Williams), 52 (by Jim Reed), 54 (by Jerry Girvin), 57 (by Lovett Williams); S. A. Grimes, 16; Professor Charles E. Huntington, Bowdoin College, 82; Karl H. Maslowski, 42; Peter and Stephen Maslowski, 56; National Park Service, 83; Outdoor Oklahoma Magazine (by Mickey Brown), 31, 63; Outdoor Photographers League Photo by John Calkins, 37; Outdoor Photographers League Photo by C. G. Maxwell, 24, 27, 67, 77; Outdoor Photographers League Photo by Don Shiner, 30, 61; W. M. Pierce, 84; Len Rue, Jr., 15, 44–45; Leonard Lee Rue III, 41; C. S. Stanwood, 36; John Watson, 50, 66, 79; F. C. Willard, 35.

Quotations on pages 32 and 33 used by permission of Harper & Row, Publishers, from *King Solomon's Ring* by Konrad Z. Lorenz, Thomas Y. Crowell Company, copyright 1952.

Quotation on page 73 used by permission of Reverend Whitney Dough from his book *Fowl Play* (Messages, Inc., P.O. Box 77, Orlando, Florida 32802, $2.50).

1    2    3    4    5    6    7    8    9    10

Library of Congress Cataloging in Publication Data

Blassingame, Wyatt.
    Wonders of crows.

    Includes index.
    SUMMARY: Discusses the origin, characteristics, habits, and enemies of the crow. Also briefly describes the care of a pet crow.
    1. Crows—Juvenile literature. [1. Crows]
I. Title.
QL696.P2367B43          598.8'64          78–21633
ISBN 0–396–07649–1

For Jeannie with love

# CONTENTS

*Queenie the dog, Jim Anderson, and Johnny the crow*

# 1

# Two Pet Crows

One September morning in Anna Maria, Florida, students in the small island school were disturbed by a loud knocking on the window. Everyone turned to look. "Why," said one girl, "it's—it's a crow!"

From the other side of the room Stuart and Jim Anderson said at the same time, "That's Johnny, our crow! What are you doing here, Johnny?"

Mrs. Clyde Phelps, the teacher and an ardent bird lover, had already heard about Johnny. "Is that your pet crow, Stuart?"

"Yes, Ma'am."

"Well, let it in," Mrs. Phelps said.

Stuart opened the window. "Come in, Johnny."

Johnny stepped in, flew across the room one time to size up the situation, then flew back to Jim Anderson's desk. He cocked his head to one side, black eyes aglitter. Then, as if to test the situation, he flew to the teacher's desk, picked up a sheet of paper in his bill, walked across the desk and dropped the paper in a wastebasket. Turning, Johnny cocked his head to one side again and eyed Mrs. Phelps.

"Crows," Mrs. Phelps told the class, "are highly intelligent birds. They have a great deal of curiosity. In this way they are almost like raccoons." And she went on to give the class a lesson about birds in general and crows in particular.

*Andy was jealous of a neighbor's cat.*

In Lewes, Delaware, young Whitney Dough sat straight upright in church. He was a seriously religious youngster; he sang in the choir, and in time he would become a Methodist minister. Now, sitting in the choir loft, he listened to the service with as close attention as a young boy can. There was the reading of the Lesson, the Gloria Patri. The minister announced his text and paused impressively.

From an open window a voice shouted hoarsely, "Hot dawg!"

The minister had opened his mouth to begin, but no sound came from it. The congregation sat absolutely silent, stunned. No one in the church knew where the voice had come from— but young Whitney Dough had ideas. That morning he had

10

forgotten to fasten Andy, his pet crow, in its cage when he left for church. Looking, he saw that a church window was open from the top, and perched in the opening was Andy.

Soon the minister and congregation saw him also. Someone waved an arm to shoo Andy away, but the bird was well out of reach and not about to be frightened. He sat happily gazing down on the people. And the minister, who knew about the pet crow from hearsay, began his sermon.

Andy listened briefly, then roared, "Quiet! Quiet!"

It was a long service for both the minister and young Whitney Dough. When at last it ended, Whitney came out to find Andy perched atop an automobile, surrounded by admirers. "I never enjoyed church so much in my life," one of them said.

Andy flew over to light on Whitney's shoulder. "Hot dawg!" he cried.

Silently Whitney swore that never again would he forget to fasten Andy in his cage on a Sunday morning.

There'll be more on the personal stories of Johnny and Andy. But first some information on crows in general.

# 2

# Crows and History

There are more than eight thousand species of birds in the world. And of all these, from one end of the earth to the other, the crows or their close relatives, the ravens, rooks, and jackdaws, are probably better known than any other family of birds. There is a common saying that if a person knows only three birds in all the world, one of these will be the crow.

Scientifically the common crow is called *Corvus brachyrhynchos*. Its closest relatives, all black, shiny, and very much alike, have the same scientific first name, *Corvus*. In fact, in common usage the word crow is often applied to all of them. And one species or another, they are found in practically every part of the world except New Zealand.

Men and corvines—as all the *Corvus* relatives are called— have had a long and close relationship. It hasn't, however, always been a happy one. Many human beings hate crows because of their ability to destroy gardens, orchards, and sometimes the nests of other birds. Other persons prize crows because they also destroy great numbers of insects and so help the same farmer they harm at other times. But even the people who hate crows

*All species of crows look pretty much alike, with shiny black feathers. Only their sizes differ slightly.*

have to admire their intelligence. And the more one knows about them, the more they are admired.

According to the Bible, the first bird that Noah sent from the ark to search for land was a member of the crow family, a raven. But if the raven found land, it must have stayed there. At least there is no mention of it returning to the ark.

The Old Testament also tells that when the Prophet Elijah was hiding in the wilderness, God commanded the ravens to feed him. "And the ravens brought him bread and flesh in the morning and bread and flesh in the evening."

According to Roman mythology, ravens were once as white as swans. But when one brought bad news to the god Apollo, the god "Blacked the raven o'er, and bid him prate in his white plumes no more." Probably it is this dark, funeral-like color, along with the harsh voice, that has made the raven and crow often symbolize evil or bad luck. In Norse mythology the raven was the bird of Odin, the god of war. It soared over the battlefields and fed on the bodies of the dead.

Shakespeare wrote in the play *Macbeth*:

> The raven himself is hoarse
> That croaks the fatal entrance of Duncan
> Under my battlements.

Probably the most famous poem about a corvine is Edgar Allan Poe's *The Raven*. In this a poet, alone, late at night, is thinking of his dead sweetheart. There is a tapping at his window. He opens it and a raven flies in to perch on a statue above his door. It makes only one sound, the word, "Nevermore." The poem ends:

> And the Raven, never flitting, still is sitting, still is sitting
> On the pallid bust of Pallas just above my chamber door;

*A raven—made famous by Edgar Allan Poe*

And his eyes have all the seeming of a demon's that is
   dreaming,
And the lamp-light o'er him streaming throws his shadow
   on the floor;
And my soul from out that shadow that lies floating on the
   floor
Shall be lifted—nevermore!

Crows and their relatives not only have become part of litera-

*Crows commonly build their nests near the tops of tall trees. This is why the lookout position near the top of a ship's mast is called the crow's nest.*

ture, they have added words to the language. Crows often build their nests near the very tops of trees, and so the lookout's shelter at the top of a ship's mast is called the crow's nest. The crow's voice is loud and harsh; to "crow over" something means to brag loudly about it.

The expression "to eat crow" means to take back what you have said. According to legend, this expression was started by an odd happening during the War of 1812. An American hunter shot a crow that fell near an unarmed British officer. The officer, by trickery, got hold of the hunter's gun and then forced the hunter to take a bite of the crow. When the officer returned the hunter's gun, the hunter then forced the officer to eat the rest of the crow. At least, that's the story.

Actually, crows are good to eat—picked and cooked, of course, not raw. John James Audubon, the great naturalist and artist, considered them a delicacy. On the other hand, crows are not always easy to prepare for cooking. My brother once decided to eat a crow he had shot. But every time he went to pick the bird's feathers with one hand, he had to squeeze its body tightly with the other hand to hold it. And every time he squeezed, air was forced through the crow's voice box, and the dead bird would cry what sounded like, "No! No!"

My brother never did eat that crow.

Crows are not the only corvines to add words to the English language. In Britain, the rooks (*Corvus frugilegus*) often nest together in great numbers. And so such a place now is called a rookery no matter what species of bird lives there. And since all corvines have a habit of grabbing up bright objects and flying off with them (more about this in the chapter on pets), the word rookery sometimes means a place where human thieves live close together.

Then there is the bird's appetite. Corvines can, and do, eat almost anything. So we have the word ravenous, meaning extremely hungry, greedy. And the verb "to raven" (sometimes it's spelled ravin) that means not only to eat hungrily but to catch and destroy its prey.

Obviously the crow family has impressed the human beings around whom it lives. And the more we know about crows, the easier this is to understand. For crows are extremely intelligent, remarkable, interesting birds well worth knowing about.

# 3

# From Reptile to Bird

A black-feathered crow, calling from the top of a tall tree, doesn't look much like a lizard crawling along the ground. Yet in the amazing story of evolution, the reptile is the ancestor of the bird.

Scientists studying the plants and animals that existed on earth millions of years ago must rely largely on the discovery of fossils. These are the remains—a skeleton, or maybe just the outline—of something preserved in ancient rock or earth. The fragile bones of a bird, however, rarely become fossils, and so for a long while scientists had little to work with. Even today much remains to be learned about the evolution of birds.

The first great discovery occurred in 1861 when a German stonecutter accidentally found a fossil dating from what scientists call the late Jurassic period, about 140 million years ago. This fossil looked strangely like both a bird and a lizard. Its head was shaped like that of a reptile, and so was its tail. Its jaws had small teeth, and its forelegs, or wings, were tipped with claws. But instead of scales, it had feathers. And the feathers were exactly like those of modern birds!

That was not all. The feet of the fossil, like those of most modern birds, had one toe pointing backward, so it could get a good grip on a tree limb. Also, its collarbone, though not yet as

*This is how* Archaeopteryx *"ancient wing" must have looked. Its forelegs have developed feathers and become true wings. But the wings still have a reptile's claws along the sides, and it could both glide through the air and climb trees.*

strong as the wishbone of a bird, was shaped like one. And without this type of wishbone a bird could never develop the powerful wing muscles attached to it.

Paleontologists—the men and women who study fossils—called this part-reptile, part-bird *Archaeopteryx*, meaning "ancient wing," and its discovery helped them understand how birds had developed from reptiles.

Even so, exactly how this was done is still unknown, though part of it can be guessed at. Some 200 million years ago when reptiles ruled the earth, not all of them were as big as the giant dinosaurs and crocodilians. Many were quite small; probably some of these began to climb plants and trees in search of food. Some developed claws as an aid to climbing. Jumping from limb to limb, some must have developed the ability to glide before they could actually fly. "Ancient wing" must have been one of

19

these since its wishbone was not yet strong enough to support the muscles needed for true flight.

Two of the physical qualities most needed for flight are light but powerful bones, and feathers. Basically a bird's skeleton is much like that of other animals—but with one big difference. Most of a bird's bones are hollow, and instead of being filled with a heavy marrow many of them contain air sacs that branch out from the lungs. Engineers building modern aircraft have learned that, pound for pound, hollow tubes are often the strongest possible design.

Even so, a bird's flight would be impossible without feathers. And how did these develop from the scales of a reptile?

*These sketches show the growth of a feather as compared to that of a reptile's scale. The first two sketches from the left show the feather rising in a hump, much as does the scale—the last picture to the right. But the feather—the third picture from the left—breaks clear of the surface. The scale remains firmly attached.*

No one can yet say for sure, but several things suggest a way. The feet of most modern birds are still covered by scales—and the chemical content of these scales and that of the bird's feathers is almost the same. Also, the scales and the feathers start to grow from the skin in the same way. Later, the feather will push clear of the skin; the scale stays closely attached. But until the feather develops, it and a scale are very much alike. Also, when scales begin to fray, as they often do, they may show a very feather-like pattern.

And so some paleontologists believe that feathers started out as frayed scales. Probably, at first, these downy feathers served only to keep the bird-reptile warm. After countless generations of short hops and longer glides, the flight feathers may have developed, and the ancient reptile became a true bird.

# 4

# How Smart Is the Crow?

Just where the crow fits into the story of bird evolution no one can say exactly. Probably, as time is measured in these matters, it was quite recent. Many ornithologists, persons who spend their lives studying birds, believe the crow family is not only one of the newest, but also the smartest of all bird families. And for anyone who has studied them, this is easy to believe.

As a group, birds are not very smart. They are "birdbrained," as the expression goes. Most of their actions are guided by instinct, by some inherent reaction rather than by the power to reason.

Corvines, however, are truly remarkable birds. A famous naturalist once wrote that if men could grow feathers and fly, very few of them would be smart enough to be crows.

Where I live on an island off the west coast of Florida, crows are common and quite tame. If I feed the sea gulls the crows join with them, circling and cawing within a few feet of me. Sometimes a dozen or more crows will descend on the cedar tree in my yard to eat the berries. I can walk directly under the tree without disturbing them at all. But one day when I saw a rat stealing seed from the bird feeder, I took my rifle and slipped quietly out the door. My intention was to shoot the rat. But the instant I came outside carrying the rifle there was a loud scream from the crows and they were gone, all of them, in one mad rush.

Where these crows, or any one of them, had seen a gun before I don't know. The island is a bird sanctuary. If birds are ever shot here, it is certainly very seldom. Yet these crows recognized a gun and its threat. To make sure it was the gun that frightened them, I repeated the experiment several times in the next few days. If I came out of the house without a gun the crows did not notice me. If I came out with a gun they were gone instantly.

This ability to recognize the danger of guns is not limited to our local crows. Persons who hunt crows, or merely watch them, have long been aware of the bird's ability to recognize danger.

Crows very often feed in large flocks. When they do, one or two are posted as lookouts. Just how the crows decide which

*When crows are feeding, one or more are always posted as lookouts for danger.*

bird will draw lookout duty is unknown. These may be the older, wiser crows with more experience of danger. But the lookout is easy to spot. Usually this bird will be at the very top of a tree, or on a post in the open where it can see in every direction. At the first sign of danger it sounds an alarm. Crows have many different cries with obviously different meanings. The lookout may merely call an alert. "Be careful!" But if it gives the danger cry, every bird in the flock is gone.

One group of scientists working with *Corvus corax*, the common American raven, taught them to count. The scientists put food in a box that had from two to six dots on the lid. Then a light would be flashed between two and six times. If the bird matched the number of flashes with the number of dots on the

*Crows seem to be more intelligent than other birds. This pet crow has learned to untie and take out a shoelace.*

lid, then it opened the right box and got food. It didn't take the ravens long to learn.

Crows also have been taught to recognize and match written figures. In this case scientists used boxes that had numbers written on them. Food would be put in one box. Then the crows would be shown a card on which was written the number of the box holding the food. Before long the crows were opening the right box every time.

Other crows have been taught to match squares, triangles, and circles to get food. Some ornithologists still believe that no bird has the actual power to reason, to think out and solve complex problems for itself. On the other hand, many scientists now believe the crow can and does solve problems by reason. Take the case of the hungry crow that watched while a fisherman cut holes through the ice of a frozen lake, then baited and dropped fishing lines into the holes.

As soon as the fisherman left the lake, the crow flew down and lit beside one of the holes. It walked slowly around it, looking in. Then it picked up the fishing line in its mouth and backed away from the hole, pulling the baited hook toward the surface. But when the crow let go the line to return to the hole, the baited hook slid down into the water. Again the crow took the line in its bill and backed away. But this time when it returned to the hole, it walked step by step on the fishing line so it could not slip. At the hole's edge the crow once more took the line in its beak, pulled the baited hook onto the ice, and ate the bait.

Similar stories have been reported by so many persons from so many parts of the world that there can be no doubt they have taken place. It is possible, of course, that sometime in the past one crow learned to do this by accident, and other crows learned by watching. But one famous ornithologist tells of a pet crow taken ice fishing by its owner. This pet crow had never been around other birds, and had never been taken fishing before. It

25

watched as its owner set his lines. On each line there was a device that made a small flag snap upright when the line was pulled. The crow watched carefully, jumped off its owner's shoulder, and ran from one line to another, making all the flags snap up. Then the crow set up a noise "that could only be laughter." And anyone who has been around pet crows knows they can laugh.

Perhaps the strangest story of bird intelligence occurred in England a few years ago. Persons began to notice that the bottles left on their doorsteps by the milkman were being opened each morning. A little bit of the top cream was gone, but only a little. At first this occurred only in one small neighborhood. Then the thefts began to spread. Soon Englishmen from one part of the country to another were being robbed of their morning cream.

An early morning observer solved the mystery. Birds had learned to pry the paper lids off the milk bottles, then drink as much of the cream as they could reach. The first bird seen doing this was a species called the blue tit, and it may have been some very smart tit that first learned how to open the bottles. (The intelligence of birds, like that of people, may vary from one individual to another.) But whatever species first opened a bottle, the crows and ravens and rooks soon learned the secret. They turned it into a nationwide crime wave. In flocks, they began to follow the milk wagons along the streets. Eventually the dairy people had to invent a new and crow-proof bottle cap.

There is an ancient Greek legend about a thirsty crow that found a bottle with a little bit of water in the bottom. But the neck of the bottle was small and the crow could not reach the water. Instead, it picked up and dropped pebbles into the bottle until the water was high enough to reach.

In England, no one reported seeing a crow drop pebbles into a milk bottle after it had drunk the top of the cream. But maybe the crows found it easier just to open another bottle.

26

*Crows are mischievous by nature. Both pet and wild crows have been known to steal clothespins, apparently for the pleasure of watching the clothes fall on the ground.*

### STRANGE ADDICTED BEHAVIOR

Yet smart as the crow is, it can sometimes do apparently stupid things. Many species of birds have been known to attack their own reflections in glass windows or even in hubcaps of automobiles. Probably this is simply an attempt to defend what the bird believes to be its own home territory from a stranger. But crows, and particularly the carrion crow (*Corvus corone*) of England, sometimes carry this to a wild extreme.

Every morning for over a week, one carrion crow hurled itself against the same window of a home in south England. With all its strength the bird flew into the window, battering it with its wings, clawing and pecking, until it fell to the ground. Then it

27

would walk back to the same spot from which it had started its first attack, *caw* once or twice, and once more hurl itself against its own reflection. For over an hour the crow kept this up, until the window was covered with its own blood and saliva. Finally it quit, apparently too weary to fight any more. Next morning, however, the crow was back again. And again each attack was exactly like those of the day before, the bird crashing against the window, falling, then walking back to the same spot to launch another attack.

This kept up for over a week, then the crow disappeared. Quite possibly it had died of weakness.

Most ornithologists believe this to have been simply an abnormal defense of its territory against the strange bird represented by its reflection. I once saw a cardinal hurl itself against a window until I hung up a curtain so the bird could no longer see its reflection. Immediately it quit fighting and went quietly about more normal business. But what of a carrion crow that attacked a window even after planks had been put up so the bird could not see its reflection? There was one small gap between the planks, and the bird seemed to know that waiting back there somewhere was its enemy. It would squeeze its way through the gap in the planks and once more begin its attack on the window.

Some ornithologists believe that some birds, like some people, simply are not normal. They become addicted to behavior they cannot stop, even knowing it to be harmful. Human beings may become addicted to smoking, alcohol, drugs. Perhaps now and then, a crow or any other bird may become addicted to total warfare against what it considers to be an enemy.

# 5

# The Uncommon Common Crow

Most ornithologists divide the North American crow into three species: the common crow (*Corvus brachyrhynchos*), the northwestern crow (*Corvus caurinus*), and the fish crow (*Corvus ossifragus*). Some scientists, however, divide the common crow (*Corvus brachyrhynchos*) into four subspecies. This way there are the eastern crow (*Corvus brachyrhynchos brachyrhynchos*), the southern crow (*Corvus brachyrhynchos paulus*), the Florida crow (*Corvus brachyrhynchos pascuus*), and the western crow (*Corvus brachyrhynchos hesperis*). But aside from where they live, the main difference among these subspecies is a slight variation in size—a difference that's scarcely as long as their scientific names.

A fully grown eastern crow, the biggest of the lot, will measure about 17 inches from the tip of its bill to the tip of its tail. The northwestern crow, the smallest American corvine, is about 14½ inches long. A very careful observer can sometimes tell one species from another by the shape of the tail or bill, but to most people a crow is a crow. This book will first lump them all together, with some later mention of how the species differ.

*Portrait of a crow, showing head detail*

## COURTSHIP

When a young male crow "falls in love" its actions are much like those of a teen-aged human being in the same condition: it sets out to make itself look as handsome, important, and attractive as possible. If the female of its choice is nearby, the male puffs out all its feathers, spreads its wings and tail, holds its head proudly high. It can actually "strut"—there's no other word for it—up and down a tree limb or on the ground. It takes to the air, whirling, diving, flashing close past the female.

As a rule the crow's voice sounds a good bit like an old-fashioned, hand-squeezed automobile horn. Yet during all the male's showmanship he is quite likely to be singing. At least it probably sounds like singing to the lady crow. Strutting around her, bobbing his head up and down, the male makes a long series of rattling noises, very different from most of the crows' calls. Often it is followed by a soft *coo-coo*, much like that of a

30

pigeon, a surprisingly gentle sound to come out of a crow.

During the early stages of the male's courtship, the female, like many a human schoolgirl, may pretend to be completely unaware of her suitor. She does not look directly at him. She turns her head away. She may fly off a short distance, and the male follows. On the other hand, if she really has no interest, he seems to realize this quickly and goes looking for someone else.

Where two males are courting the same female and she shows no definite preference, this may lead to warfare. The two males clash in midair, each trying to rise above the other. They batter at one another with wings and bills. Sometimes they become so

*Male crows show off for a female when courting.*

intent on fighting they fall, hit the ground and roll about, still fighting. Actually, however, little damage is done. The weaker bird gives up and leaves.

It is probable that a good part of the male's courtship is intended to impress the female with his ability to find and defend a nesting site. If she is impressed, if she in her turn "falls in love," she signals her acceptance by squatting in front of the male, half raising her wings, spreading her tail, and quivering all her feathers. She may open her bill and make small chirping sounds, looking exactly like a baby bird waiting to be fed. The male in turn will present her with any choice item of food he has found.

It may sound odd to speak of birds falling in love. Many serious ornithologists, however, believe that among the corvines and some other birds there is something beyond a mere sexual drive—a true, honest affection of one bird for the other.

The most careful, scientific study that has ever been made of a corvine's sex life was by Dr. Konrad Lorenz, a German naturalist. Dr. Lorenz raised many generations of jackdaws (*Corvus monedula*) in his home, giving them complete freedom to come and go as they wished. In a wonderful book called *King Solomon's Ring* he wrote about the things he had learned.

Not only do jackdaws mate for life, Dr. Lorenz learned, but they become "engaged" before they "marry." Jackdaws are not sexually mature and able to mate until their second year. Yet they pair off, become "engaged," a full year before that. From that time on, "hardly ever separated by more than a yard, the two make their way through life. . . . It is really touching to see how affectionate these two wild creatures are with each other. Every delicacy that the male finds is given to his bride and she accepts it with the plaintive, begging gestures and notes otherwise typical of baby birds."

The most touching part of the birds' relationship, Dr. Lorenz wrote, was that "their affection increases with the years. . . . Even after many years the male still feeds his wife with the same solicitous care, and finds for her the same low tones of love, tremulous with inward emotion, that he whispered in his first spring of betrothal and of life."

No equally detailed study has been made of *Corvus brachyrhynchos*, the common American crow. But it is believed that they also mate for life. Certainly the male crow courts his lady exactly as does the jackdaw. Quite possibly he remains as much "in love" throughout his life.

In his book, Dr. Lorenz explains that when he writes of "love" among jackdaws and some other animals, he is not trying to give them human emotions. Instead, he writes, "I am trying to show you what an enormous animal inheritance remains in man to this day."

THE NEST AND EGGS

After the male and female crow have paired off, their first occupation is to find the proper site for a nest. In an area where there are plenty of trees, the birds are most likely to choose a tall one. The nest is usually in a fork very near the top; however, the limb must be big and strong enough to hold considerable weight.

But crows are found in many parts of the world where trees are scarce or even nonexistent. Here, if the crow could not fit itself to its surroundings, it could not exist. The ability to adapt is one measure of intelligence, and the intelligent crow, like the intelligent raccoon, changes its habits to fit its needs. In some parts of western Canada where there are no trees at all, crows may make their nests in low bushes, in the reeds around a lake, or even on the ground. On the Great Plains of the United States, crows often nest in the trees that border small streams. And if there are no trees, they may build nests on the crossbars of telephone and power lines. The birds sometimes use bits of barbed wire from fences to work into the nests. Sometimes this short circuits the power line—and probably the crow also. In fact, one Midwestern power company is said to spend over $5,000 each year trying to keep the crows from nesting on its poles. In mountain country crows have been known to nest on rocky ledges, and at least one pair built its nest on top of the chimney of a country church.

Wherever nests are built, both male and female crow take a part in the work. Since it is difficult and sometimes impossible to tell one bird from the other, just how the job is divided is uncertain. Usually the male seems to do most of the fetching of material, while the female arranges it to suit her taste. Most often the work is done in the mornings, the birds taking the afternoons off to rest and feed. From start to finish the job takes about twelve to fourteen days.

From the outside most crows' nests look alike. Almost but not quite round, they are usually about two feet across. From the bottom of the base to the top of the outside rim, it is about eight or nine inches. The cup in which the eggs are laid and where the babies hatch is about six to seven inches across and four to five inches deep.

From below the nest looks like an untidy pile of twigs, sticks, string, leaves, whatever is available. Sometimes the base is made of sticks almost a foot-and-a-half long and a half inch thick. The inside cup, however, is a beautifully finished piece of work. And this seems to be the job of the female alone. Standing in the nest, she may weave together soft strips of bark the male has torn from trees. Or she may line the nest with moss or old rags or bits of wool. Nests have been found lined completely with hair from a deer's tail, others with the hair of rabbits. Whatever its lining, the bowl of the nest is soft, compact, and well built.

Crows normally lay four to six eggs, but both the number and

34

*The nest of white-necked ravens in Arizona*

the color may vary. Usually the eggs are greenish, or bluish-green, and splotched with brown and gray markings. Sometimes an egg may have so much brown it is almost red, but this is rare.

Both parents take turns incubating the eggs. In fact, both parents have been seen sitting on the nest at the same time. This may have been a gesture of affection, or it may be that one bird merely picked this spot to rest for awhile. Certainly it crowded the nest.

The nesting crow develops what ornithologists call a brood patch: the bird loses most of the feathers on its body where it touches the eggs. This allows the heat of the parent's body to pass directly to the eggs, keeping them at a warm 93 to 95 degrees.

35

*A common crow less than a week old*

### The Young

After eighteen to twenty days the baby bird inside the egg is fully formed. It is a pale pink, or flesh color, with tiny, dark tufts of down on its head, back, and wings. Its eyes are still closed. Near the tip of its small bill there is a small bump of hard, bonelike material called an egg tooth. With this the baby bird, instinctively struggling toward freedom, cracks its shell and wiggles free. Usually the parent crow eats what is left of the shell, or throws it out of the nest.

Within a day or two of birth the egg tooth breaks off the baby's bill. After five days the round, dark eyes are open and the skin, still barely touched with feathers, is turning brown. Another five days and the feathers are growing rapidly. Up to this time the babies have remained fairly quiet, but now their mouths are open wider than their eyes and they keep up an

36

almost constant squawking for food. Both parents are flying back and forth bringing insects, worms, bits of meat torn from dead animals, fruit, berries, anything they can find. Apparently the babies never think it is enough. They keep calling for more. The inside of a baby crow's mouth is a bright orange-red. Look into a nest where six youngsters are squalling for food and all you can see are open mouths.

Adult crows frequently rob the nests of other birds, eating either the eggs or young. But this is not altogether a one-sided affair. Baby crows keep up such a clamor for food that any passing hawk or raccoon, cat or snake, is more than likely to hear them. Then the baby crow is apt to be eaten in turn.

*The mouth of the baby crow looks as if it were lined with red flannel. Later this red will disappear.*

*The red-shouldered hawk has been known to kill a grown crow, but crows, working together, will usually drive off a hawk.*

Young crows have one very neat habit they share with certain birds of prey. They do not foul their own nest. As soon as it is able to move about, long before it can fly, the baby will struggle to the edge of the nest, then turn its tail so that the droppings fall outside the nest.

By the time the crow is four weeks old, it has most of its feathers. On the back these have a slightly grayish tone, not quite as shiny black as they will be later, but the wings and tail already glitter in the sun. And it is about this time that the young crow seems to become aware, almost suddenly, of two things: that it is a crow, and that a crow must be afraid of many things. Baby crows that fall from their nests before they are able to fly often appear to be totally without fear. They have been seen to toddle happily up to a hungry cat, or to a person, mouth open and waiting to be fed. Yet this same bird, left in its nest until able to fly a few days later, would be completely wild and unapproachable.

# 6

# Migration

Even after the young birds have left the nest, the crow family stays together for awhile. The parents feed the young and, at the same time, teach them to hunt for themselves. And there are times when, at least to the human observer, it looks as if the adult birds are teaching the young about flying—not *how* to fly, since the young are already flying, but how to enjoy flying.

Usually the birds choose a time when a strong wind is blowing. Or it may be a place where the air currents change sharply at the crest of a hill or above a steep cliff. Here one bird, then another, will swoop, whirl, turn completely over, fold its wings and fall fifty feet or more, then spin upward again. This may be a game of follow-the-leader, played for pure pleasure, or it may be the adult birds are indeed teaching the young the marvelous things that can be done with a pair of wings. Whatever the reason, the crows seem to have a wonderful time.

Most scientists now believe that a bird's migratory instinct is touched off by the amount of sunlight it is exposed to daily. As

*Notice that the tails of these young crows are still a bit ragged. They will fill out and become rounded as the birds age.*

*A crow about to land*

days grow longer in the spring, the bird's instinct prepares it to fly north; when days grow short in the fall, instinct moves the bird to fly south. Also it is known that the increasing amount of spring sunlight has an effect on the birds' sex organs: it causes them to mature and become ready for summer mating.

But what if the amount of sunlight to which the bird is exposed is changed artificially, at the wrong time of the year?

A Canadian ornithologist kept a number of crows in an outdoor aviary. Here they were exposed to temperatures as low as 44 degrees Fahrenheit below zero. But starting early in November, when the days should have been getting shorter, the scientist turned on lights earlier and earlier each day. By January the crows were getting as much light each day as, in the wild, they would have had in April.

They began to grow restless and show signs of wanting to migrate. Tests showed their sex organs had become fully mature, ready for mating. So now the scientist released the birds, watching to see what would happen.

Half the crows flew north, as if it were spring. Half flew south, as if it were fall. And no one knew why.

Migration among crows is a very curious thing anyway. During the summer months most crows live in pairs, or families. One family may join another for awhile where food is plentiful, but during these months it is very unusual to see any huge number of crows together.

However, beginning in the fall and early winter, more and more crows will often roost together at night. Both the migratory instinct and the everlasting search for food seem to play a part. Southern crows don't migrate very much, and the population stays the same pretty much the year round. In some areas where both food and roosting places are plentiful, crows seldom gather in huge numbers. But in many places the ground may be frozen or snow-covered, the food scarce. Along the coasts and near big waterways, food may be more available. So often crows move toward large bodies of water.

In the Midwest, abandoned cornfields may still be scattered with grain. In such places the crows establish roosts where at first the birds may number only a few dozen, then hundreds, then thousands upon thousands.

Many species of migrating birds leave an area entirely, flying hundreds or thousands of miles south for the winter, north for summer breeding. Some crows do this also. Scientists have learned that many of the crows wintering in the central United States spend their summers in Canada. But in the eastern United States, the winter migration seems to be a local shifting rather than true migration: some crows from Maine and New Hampshire may move into Massachusetts, and some from Massachusetts move to Connecticut and New York, and some from New York go to New Jersey. These crows do not usually go far

*A crow roost in the early evening as the birds begin to gather. Most of these are perched near the tops of trees, but as more birds arrive many will move to lower limbs.*

enough to change the climate in which they winter. But they do gather to roost together at night in almost incredible numbers.

Dr. C. W. Townsend, an ornithologist, once spent many hours studying such a roosting place near Ipswich Beach, Massachusetts. Here thousands of crows spent each night in a thicket of evergreen trees surrounded by a few other dead or leafless trees.

Every winter afternoon, starting several hours before dark, these crows began to assemble. They came in three black, flowing rivers of birds, from the north, west, south, from every direction except the open sea. Usually the wind was from the north, cold and strong. Most of the birds, especially those coming up from the south, kept low, flying with slow, strong wingbeats. They took advantage of dunes along the beach, of trees, of any protection from the wind. Also these early birds, those that began to arrive by two or three o'clock in the afternoon, did not

fly directly to the roost. Instead, they paused to rest in the shelter of dunes, to search for food, then little by little move closer to the roost.

Gradually the dunes as well as the sky began to blacken with birds. The air was filled with their cawing. Now and then a hundred or more would whirl like a cloud into the air, circle, and land again a few hundred feet from where they had been. Slowly the great mass of birds moved closer to the roost.

"About sunset," Dr. Townsend wrote, "a great tumult of corvine voices issued from the multitude—a loud cawing with occasional wailing notes—and a black cloud rose into the air and settled into the branches of the bare trees to the west of the roost. From here as it was growing dusk they glided into the evergreens for the night."

Some naturalists believe that the first crows to approach the roost are the wisest and oldest birds in the flock. They are the scouts, making sure the roost is safe for the night, and that the other birds do not come in until the scouts give an all-safe signal. This may be true. Certainly if these first arrivals sight an enemy, they set up a cry that alerts the entire flock—as many crow hunters, both human and nonhuman, have found out.

The crows that Dr. Townsend was watching left their roost in the morning more rapidly than they had gathered the night before. Dr. Townsend, gloved and overcoated against the zero degree weather, huddled against a tree to watch.

It was still completely dark when he heard the birds overhead begin to stir. Now and then there would be a short flapping of wings, a harsh *caw*, as some bird moved from one spot to another. Some of them may have flown away even before it was light enough for Dr. Townsend to see. Certainly with the first light he saw a small flight of birds lift into the sky. At about half past six, with the first faint glow of the rising sun, there was "a great uproar of *caws* and *uks*, occasionally rattles and wailing *ahhhs*, a broad stream boiled up from the roosting trees and spread off toward the west . . . Then no more flew away for five minutes although the tumult in the roost continued in increasing volume. At 6:40 the roost boiled over again but the birds spreading in all directions soon united into a black river that flowed over the dunes . . ." The sun rose at 7:14, and by now almost all the birds were gone. Even so, Dr. Townsend wrote, a few "were still dozing in the evergreens."

# 7

# The Voice of the Crow

About 1900 years ago, a Roman called Pliny the Elder wrote a book called *Natural History*. Today some naturalists say the book should have been called *Unnatural History* because of its many errors. And perhaps the worst of them dealt with the voice of the crow.

Pliny wrote that if the tongue of a crow was split, it could then learn to talk. And for 1900 years, many persons have been quoting this and believing it. But the truth is that if you cut a crow's tongue, it will not help the bird to talk. Instead, more than likely the crow will bleed to death.

Now it is true that some crows, like some parrots and parakeets, can learn to say human words. And just as with parrots and parakeets, some crows learn more quickly than others. But all of them learn without having their tongues cut.

Certainly the crow is not regarded as a songbird. Most persons think of it as making a loud, harsh cawing noise and nothing else. Actually the crow has a rather remarkable voice range even though it isn't musical. The *caw* for which the crow is best known can be given in many ways, with various tones and rhythms. One ornithologist timed the simple *caw* call of the crow in four different rhythms. One was *caw caw caw*. Another was *caw caw*, then a pause, and again *caw caw*. Another was *caw*

Crows are noisy, constantly calling to one another, or, from a safe distance, scolding a possible enemy such as a cat or dog. This one is shouting at a cat on the ground below.

*This crow seems not to mind the cat sitting on the fence below him.*

*caw* pause, and a single *caw*. Still another was *caw caw*, pause, *caw*, pause, and *caw*.

All of these variations seem to have meaning to crows. When a flock of crows is feeding and their lookout cries *caw c-a-aw!*, every bird in hearing takes wing. Yet that same lookout may cry *caw caw caw* in a slightly different way, and the feeding birds don't look up, since apparently the cry has meant, "All's well." The alarm *caw c-a-aw!* has an obviously excited note. When crows join in mob attack on their enemy the great horned owl, then every crow in the flight seems to scream at the top of its lungs, a truly frenzied cry that can't be mistaken. And, as mentioned earlier, a crow courting his lady love has a call that is almost soft, a sound that one ornithologist called "a love-sick gurgle."

Even persons who normally pay little attention to birds will sometimes notice how the voices of crows may change. I have a friend who lives in Vermont where most crows are *Corvus brachyrhynchos*, the common crow. Where I live on an island off the Gulf Coast of Florida, most of the crows are *Corvus ossifragus*, the fish crow. "Your crows," she said, "have a southern accent!"

She was right, at least in a way. Every species of crow has a voice slightly different in pitch from the others. Perhaps this is related to the fact that the various species are slightly different in size. Even so, the basic calls seem to be the same. I don't know if this has ever been scientifically tested, but I believe that a Florida fish crow, transported to the Pacific Coast of Canada, would know what his northwestern relative, *Corvus caurinus*, was talking about.

Aside from man, the great horned owl is the most deadly enemy of the crow. Able to see at night and silent in its flight, this owl often attacks crows in the roosting area.

# 8

# The Crow's Enemies

In nature crows have comparatively few enemies, and the chief of these is the great horned owl. The war between these big owls and the crows is everlasting, with each side having its own advantage. The owls' great size, their ability to see at night, and the almost total silence with which they fly make them deadly enemies after dark. In darkness the owl may swoop down on a crow's nest or roost, kill with a single stroke of its great talons, and carry its prey away to feed in peace. A single crow is no match for a great horned owl, and certainly not at night.

The crow's advantage lies in its intelligence, its ability to communicate with one another, and to work together. Crows recognize owls as enemies. When a single crow, or several crows, sight an owl by daylight it immediately sets up a wild cawing. This is a distinct cry, almost a scream, apparently meaning, "Owl! Owl! Our enemy, the owl!" Every crow in hearing distance—and this *caw* can be heard a long distance—comes rushing to the attack. Together they literally mob the owl. If it takes refuge in a tree or bush, the crows swarm around it, some a few feet away, others whirling past within inches, screaming, pecking. Occasionally a crow will actually crash into the owl from behind. But owls have extremely sensitive ears, and usually the crows' violent screaming alone will put one to flight. When finally the owl does take wing, the great mass of crows follows. They fly above the owl, between its wings, pecking at its beak and head. Only when the owl has fled well beyond the crows' living area will they leave it alone.

Just as the crow recognizes the owl as an enemy, so some of the smaller birds recognize the crow as a would-be destroyer of nests and young. So they try to drive the crow away from their nesting area. Mockingbirds, redwing blackbirds, kingbirds are all much smaller than crows, but they can fly faster and maneuver more easily. When a crow comes near their nest, they attack from above and behind, just as the crows fly after owls. Actually they do very little damage, but they do chase the crow away.

The noisy cries of baby crows may lead snakes, raccoons, and rats to their nests. Even so, only a comparatively few crows are destroyed in this way. A fox will eat a crow, if it can catch one,

*The fox may kill any crow it can surprise on the ground, but the wary and cautious crow is not easy to surprise. Crows, in turn, will mob and drive away any fox they see by daylight.*

*Frogs, lizards, and insects make up part of the wild crow's diet.*

which is seldom. On the other hand, crows like to mob a fox, or a cat, almost as much as they do owls.

But by all odds, the greatest enemy of the crow is man.

## THE WAR BETWEEN MAN AND CROW

Crows are omnivorous—they will, and do, eat almost anything. And lots of it. In many places crows are considered scavengers, almost like buzzards, feeding on the remains of animals killed along the highways. Or they will feed on living animals they capture for themselves, mice, insects, lizards. They rob the nests of other birds, taking either eggs or the young. Crows often build their own nests near the nesting places of ducks and geese, destroying the young water birds in large numbers. In doing so they sometimes make fierce enemies out of hunters and outdoorsmen who might otherwise be great admirers of the crow.

But it is the farmer who often has an intense, personal dislike for crows. A great flock of crows descending on an orchard of

This crow has killed a garter snake several times its own size. It may not be able to eat the snake all at once, but will probably have help from other crows.

ripening peaches, apricots, or cherries, may do thousands of dollars worth of damage in a few hours. In the Midwest crows flock to the fields where young corn is sprouting over hundreds of acres. Like an army of black-uniformed midgets, the birds march down the rows. With their bills they pull up the young plants, eat the seed from the bottom, and throw the rest away.

In fact, one farmer swore the crows followed the rows and dug up his seed corn before it had time to sprout. Trying to fool them, he used a mechanical planter. This planted each grain of corn an exact distance from the one before it, but left no row marks for the birds to follow. So the crows, the farmer said, dug around until they found one grain of corn, kept digging until they found another. Then they would look back to see how far they had come, pace off an equal distance, and dig up the next grain. The birds swept across his field, each digging up one grain, pacing off the distance, and digging up another.

That's the story. More likely, the corn had begun to sprout

*Crows love corn, on or off the cob. This one has picked up four grains before swallowing the first, a common trick of crows and other birds.*

*A crow trying to open a cereal box*

enough to make cracks in the earth visible to the bird's sharp eyes.

You might not think a crow could feed on hard-shelled pecans. It can. The bird holds the nut with its foot, breaks it open with three or four heavy blows of its bill, then eats the meat. A great flight of crows can practically wipe out a pecan grove within a few days. Crows have also been known to destroy acres of watermelons. And this was not done to feed on the melons. Most often the watermelon patches are attacked in the late afternoon when the crows are returning to their roost from a long day of dry feeding elsewhere. The crows stop at the watermelon patch. Each bird drills a hole in a melon, takes a drink of the juice, then flies on to roost, leaving the melon to rot.

When crows roost together by the thousands and tens of thousands, they may actually kill the trees in which they roost. If the roost is near a town, its odor becomes offensive. The vast number of birds may make the streets, yards, the roofs of houses filthy with their droppings. In such numbers crows become an unwanted nuisance.

Until recently there were no game laws in the United States to protect crows. It was legal to kill as many as possible at any time of the year. And often they were slaughtered in unbelievable numbers.

When a crow roost near Binger, Oklahoma, became a nuisance to the entire town, the State Game and Fish Commission was asked to destroy it. Sticks of dynamite were placed in the roosting trees, connected by wires, then all exploded at one time after the birds had settled for the night. Next morning, 18,000 dead crows were gathered and burned. Another 26,000 were dynamited in a roost near Dempsey, Oklahoma. In Collingsworth County, Texas, an estimated 40,000 crows were killed in a single roost. But the champion crow killer was probably a man named Frank Davis. Working for the Illinois State Department of Conservation, he is said to have officially destroyed 328,000 crows by dynamiting their roosts.

Despite this tremendous slaughter the total number of crows in the country was only slightly affected. When a roost was destroyed, the birds that survived simply moved elsewhere. When they roosted in smaller numbers, it was not practical to attack them with dynamite.

When a great flock of crows descended on an apricot orchard in California, the owner quickly put out some poisoned fruit with a strange result. A few crows ate the poisoned apricots and became sick. Instantly many other crows gathered around them, cawing, flapping their wings, trying to help. Then the poisoned crows died. Apparently the other crows understood what had happened. At least they left that orchard and went elsewhere for food.

There can be no doubt that crows often do tremendous damage to farm crops. But like most things in life, it is not entirely a one-sided story. In New Jersey one farmer noticed that very early every morning a great number of crows descended on the field where he had planted asparagus. So he hired men to stand in the field in the early morning and shoot crows. But the asparagus didn't grow. Examining his field one morning, the farmer found thousands upon thousands of cutworms. These lie buried during the day but come out at night to eat the roots of the plants. The early rising crows were feeding on the cutworms before they could rebury themselves. When the crows were allowed to return to the field, they cleaned up the cutworms and the asparagus crop prospered.

A farmer in Massachusetts saw crows kill one of his newborn lambs. To get rid of the crows he offered to pay a fifty cent bounty for every one that was shot. Hunters soon killed almost every crow in the neighborhood. But the next spring the grass in the farmer's pasture did not grow well. Nor the year after. Studying the matter, the farmer found that white grubs were eating the grass roots. When the crows were allowed to return, they cleaned up the grubs and the pasture recovered.

Certainly there are times when too many crows can do serious damage to both farms and towns. Also there are times when they are of benefit.

It is not an easy problem to solve.

## CROW HUNTING

In the past many hunters have not thought of the crow as a game bird like quail, ducks, doves, grouse, and others. This is chiefly because crows are not usually considered good eating, even though some persons do eat and enjoy crow meat. In recent years, however, crow hunting as a sport has become increasingly popular.

The crow is not as swift and shifty a target as a quail or dove. It can cruise at twenty miles an hour and has been known to fly, with a following wind, at sixty. But usually its flight is rather slow and steady. This, along with its size, makes it a fairly easy target for the hunter—*if* the crow has no idea there is a hunter.

Hunters find that crow shooting is more a battle of wits than a test of great skill with a gun.

The crow is extremely cautious. Hunters who have spent years studying crows believe the wise, experienced adult birds can talk to and educate the young. Since crows keep a lookout high in a tree or on a post, it is almost impossible for a hunter to sneak up on them.

*Mortal enemy of the crow, the owl—stuffed or decoy—is hoisted high in a tree to attract the black-feathered fellows.*

In this battle of wits the experienced hunter makes use of the crow's own nature. Men who have listened carefully know the calls used by crows to announce the discovery of a great horned owl or some other enemy, and they know this call will bring a rush of crows to join the fight. Many hunters have learned to make artificial crow calls which, if the hunter is skillful enough, can sound exactly like living crows. There are also taped recordings of actual crow voices that a hunter may play on a small recorder.

These devices may bring the crows flocking, but if the hunter is not truly skilled in his call the birds may catch a false note and shy away. Some hunters swear that often an old, experienced crow (the hunters call them "college crows") not only will detect a false note in the call, but will then light in a tree just out of range. From here, cawing at the top of its lungs, it will warn all the other crows.

Even if the hunter can duplicate the call of the crows absolutely, one glimpse of a man with a gun and the birds swerve out of range. So crow hunters often use camouflage suits like those of soldiers in Vietnam. Often hunters build blinds—shelters that look like bushes or a pile of old tree limbs—in which to hide. From inside the blinds, they sound their crow calls to bring the birds close.

To make the calls more effective, many hunters use decoys. Usually this is a stuffed or carved figure of a great horned owl placed high in a tree or on a post where it is easily visible. Crows rushing to answer the hunter's call watch the decoy and so are less likely to see the hunter. In fact crows sometimes attack the decoy so viciously they knock it all to pieces.

Until 1972, there were no game laws to protect crows. Hunters could not only kill as many as possible, they could shoot them at any time of year, including the nesting season. Then the U. S. Fish and Wildlife Service passed a law to protect crows

*Near Fort Cobb, Oklahoma, crows by the hundreds of thousands come to feed on peanuts left in the fields by farmers. Here a few are seen against the sunset as they return to their roosts.*

during the nesting season, the exact time to vary from state to state.

Under this law, exceptions may be made where crows in great numbers are causing trouble for farmers or town. But, use of poison or dynamite is no longer legal. Where the crows gather in great numbers, hunting with guns—some sportsmen even use bows and arrows—usually keeps them under control.

Probably the world's most famous crow hunting spot is at the Fort Cobb Reservoir in Oklahoma. Nearby farmers plant thousands of acres of peanuts each year, and even after the crops are harvested many peanuts remain in the fields. Here each fall the crows come quite literally by the millions. And here come hunters from all over the United States. They bring their decoys and their blinds to match their wits and skill against those of the crows.

Each year at Fort Cobb there is held an Annual Oklahoma Crow Barbecue, where hunters and friends feast on some of the birds that have been shot. Some consider it a real feast, others are not so certain. As one hunter said, "Crow meat is not bad— if you like barbecue sauce and put on enough."

# 9

# The Care of Baby Crows

Many persons believe that if a baby bird has been touched by human hands, its parents will no longer look after it. This is not true. It is true that if the parent birds are much disturbed while building the nest, or even while incubating the eggs, they may leave this spot and find another. But once the eggs have hatched, it takes a great deal to make the parents desert them. If you find a baby that has fallen from its nest, normally the best thing to do is to replace it in the nest. The parent birds will take care of it.

However, if you find a very young crow, want an unusual pet, and are prepared to work hard for a month or two, then adopt it. But to make a truly good pet, your baby crow should not yet be able to fly, not even a little. From his studies Dr. Konrad Lorenz decided that the very young corvine became "imprinted" with the image of its keeper and from that time on would react toward human beings as most birds do toward members of their own species. This was not true for all birds, but it was for corvines.

In the United States, a number of ornithologists tested Dr. Lorenz' theory. Among them was a Mr. A. D. Cruickshank. From one nest he took a baby crow when it was only two weeks old. He and his wife fed the baby, allowing it to see no other birds for awhile. As soon as it could walk the crow began to follow them about the house. It begged for food exactly as a wild crow might beg its parents. When it could fly, it would perch on Cruickshank's shoulder or head. Outdoors it might fly into a tree or onto a telephone pole. But very soon it came down again. The Cruickshank's home was its home and it stayed with them as long as it lived.

A short time after getting the first crow, Mr. Cruickshank captured a second one. This one had already left the nest and could fly, but only slightly. Cruickshank raised it exactly as he did the other. For two weeks it was kept by itself, seeing no other birds and no persons except the Cruickshanks. It was carefully fed by hand. But it never begged for food as the other bird did. Though it accepted food, it would otherwise cringe away from the Cruickshanks rather than follow them. And the first time it was released outdoors it flew away, never to return.

A friend of mine adopted a fish crow so young its eyes were not yet open. Soon it was following her around as it would have its own mother. If she sat down, it would climb onto her shoulder even before it could fly.

One day it was sitting on her shoulder while she worked in

*If raised together, animals that might otherwise be natural enemies can be close friends.*

*A pet crow often brings offerings of food to its owner—and the offering may be anything from a cracker to a dead mouse.*

the yard. The crow—its name was Midnight—began to flap its wings. This was an instinctive motion it had been making for some time. But now, suddenly and without understanding what was happening, Midnight found itself airborne. Cawing wildly, dipping and zigzagging, it flew across the street and banged into a tree. This knocked it to earth. Instantly it headed for home, running this time, not flying, and begging to be picked up.

In a short time Midnight became an accomplished aerialist. He could also say, "Hello!" which he often did, at the top of his lungs. One day he was in the yard when a flight of crows passed low overhead. The leader of the flight swooped down and gave the call that ornithologists believe means, "Follow me."

Midnight cocked his head, waved his wings. "Hello!" he shouted.

The crows flew on. Midnight kept following his owner about the yard.


FEEDING

A baby crow, like its parents, will eat almost anything, and a lot of it. A baby crow may be fed worms (broken into small pieces), crickets, tiny bits of raw meat, bread soaked in water or egg, small bits of fruit, almost anything you might eat yourself. The food must be kept in small fragments, and it must be kept coming. In fact, very young birds need to be fed almost every twenty minutes during the daylight hours. From dark to daylight the owner may get a little rest.

Finding natural food for one baby crow can be a full-time job for its owner. Fortunately, it is no longer necessary to feed the babies natural foods only. Purina High Protein Dog Meal makes a complete diet. If natural foods are used, a very small amount of vitamin B1 should be added now and then. With the dog meal, this is not necessary.

It is best not to give baby birds water with an eyedropper. This may work—it often does—but sometimes water given in this way goes into the bird's lungs. It is best to soak the little bit of dog meal, or whatever food is being used, in water and then drop it into the baby's mouth. Sometimes it is necessary to push the food down with a finger.

If a baby crow is to be raised by a human being, then the human parent must make an artificial nest for it. This may be no more than a cardboard box lined with soft cloth. But it must be kept warm, particularly if the baby is not yet well feathered. A small heater may be placed close by, or a constantly burning light bulb. But the temperature in the nest should be kept close to 93 degrees, or even a degree or two warmer. On the other hand, don't get the temperature too high. Too much heat can do more harm than too little. As the bird becomes more fully feathered, the temperature can be lowered.

## THE CAGE

When the young crow is big enough to leave its nest, it will hop, walk, and try to fly. At this time it will need a cage.

A crow needs a fairly large cage. This is not only because it is a large bird; it is also a very active one. A happy crow is a busy one. Even a caged crow will rarely sit still. It goes back and forth, up and down.

A good size for a crow cage is four feet long, four feet high, and two feet wide. It can be slightly smaller, or as big as you have room for.

*This pet crow has a good-sized cage*

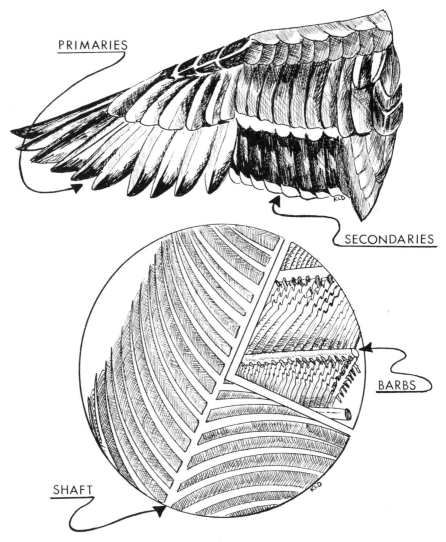

PRIMARIES

SECONDARIES

BARBS

SHAFT

*A close up of a bird's wing feathers*

Your bird will also need small toys to play with and newspapers to rip apart. For some reason crows love to rip papers. They like to hide small objects, bring them out and rehide them. A mirror with a small bell on it will keep a crow busy for hours.

The tail feathers of the young crow tend to be ragged. If the perch in your cage is so close to the end that the crow brushes its tail against the bars in turning, the tail is apt to stay ragged. This, in turn, makes flying more difficult. So the perches should be far enough from the ends of the cage for the crow to turn without touching the bars.

Sometimes it may be necessary to keep your crow from flying as well as it might. This may be done by trimming the wing feathers, but it should be done very carefully. Do *not* simply cut across the strong, bony shaft of the primaries—the long, strong feathers at the ends of the wings. In the crow these recover very slowly if at all. Instead, trim some of the small, downlike parts along the sides of the shafts of the primary feathers.

And remember. If you want your pet to talk, be patient. Repeat the word you want it to say over and over. Some crows learn much more rapidly than others. But never, NEVER, cut its tongue. It will only bleed to death.

# 10

## Johnny, Andy, and Other Pets

Whitney Dough and his mother made a point of teaching Andy, the crow, to speak. One after another they would say, "Hello. Hello," to the bird, repeating it over and over. Andy ignored them. Left to itself it would make a wide variety of crow noises, but no human sounds. Then when Andy was slightly more than a year old, he heard the next door neighbor calling her son, "Jimmee! Jimmee!"

"Hello!" Andy shouted.

Having learned one word, Andy quickly learned others. Before long he had a vocabulary of twelve to fifteen words. Also he could bark like a dog, meow like a cat, and sometimes laugh like a whole roomful of people.

Dr. Lorenz found that although many of his jackdaws could say a few words, they seemed to learn best when the words were spoken in an excited voice, or when the bird itself was excited. Once one of his pets disappeared for several weeks. Then it came home again, with a badly torn foot. And the bird itself told him what had happened. It kept saying, "Look what we caught in the trap! Look what we caught in the trap!"

In all probability the bird had heard this only once. Yet it remembered the entire sentence.

Many of Andy's words were learned more or less in the same

way. When Whitney played cops and robbers with his friends, Andy joined in the game, flying wildly back and forth. Soon he was shouting, "Hands up!" Or, "I won! I won!" Sometimes this prompted Whitney to say, "Oh, shut up!" or "Quiet!"—words that Andy quickly added to his vocabulary.

One of Andy's experiences illustrated another of Dr. Konrad Lorenz' experiments. Dr. Lorenz learned that if a young corvine is badly frightened it will never forget, or forgive, what frightened it. One of Whitney's friends had a pony and small wagon in which Andy was taken for a ride. At this time the bird's wing had been clipped and it could not fly, but it rode happily in the wagon bed. Then the pony ran away; the wagon bounced wildly and Andy was thrown out.

Twenty years later Whitney Dough, now a Methodist minister, wrote a book about his pet. In it he said: "To this day . . . the crow is thrown into a panic at the sight of a horse, or at the sound of a rattling wagon. Andy can be nonchalant of a razor-toothed, tiger-clawed feline killer, but let a wee child approach with a wee express wagon and he almost dies of heart failure!"

One of Andy's major accomplishments was playing the piano.

*Andy liked to play the piano and sing*
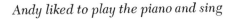

*The cover of a book by Whitney Dough about his adventures with Andy the crow*

At least he loved to walk up and down the keys. Sometimes he would stop in front of the sheet music, stare as if he could read it, and stomp his feet. It was a talent appreciated more by Whitney and his young friends than by the neighbors.

Like most crows Andy had a great curiosity, plus an overwhelming desire to steal and hide anything that took his fancy. Clotheslines had a great fascination for Andy and several times he infuriated neighboring housewives by stealing the clothespins, allowing the wet clothing to fall on the ground.

What Andy did with the clothespins remained a mystery for some time. Then one day Whitney climbed on a stepladder to hang a picture in his bedroom. To his left was an old-fashioned wardrobe that reached almost to the ceiling. Around the top of it was a small balustrade. Back of this was a great pile of clothespins, a toothbrush, one sock, seventeen cents in change, a lady's lipstick, pencils, matches, and a magnificent collection of broken glass.

74

Most ornithologists believe that because of dangers and disease, few wild crows live more than four to five years. Andy lived to be twenty-six, certainly one of the oldest crows on record. The last three years of his life he was blind. Even so he could recognize Whitney's voice. Spoken to, he would ruffle his feathers and bow his head in the same gesture of affection that wild crows make to their mates.


## JOHNNY

Stuart and Jim Anderson got their pet crow by climbing a tall tree in Homewood, Illinois. There was a nest with four baby crows in it, eyes barely open, and the boys took nest and all. Raising four crow babies was a bit too much, even for two boys, and one by one they gave away all but Johnny.

Even one baby crow, however, was one too many for Queenie, the Anderson's dog. Queenie was used to being the only pet; now a small, black, feathered creature was getting all the attention. Not only that, but it ate Queenie's dog food from right under Queenie's nose. Johnny could not fly yet, but he could peck Queenie's tail and run. Queenie regarded the little crow bleakly, then leaned over and picked it up in her mouth. Johnny squalled in outrage, but Queenie carried the bird out of the house and across the yard to the farthest corner. There she put it down, turned and came back in the house.

Johnny followed close behind.

After this Queenie accepted Johnny. They ate together from the same dish, and Johnny slept between Queenie's outstretched paws. When the Andersons moved to Florida, Johnny and Queenie were shipped together in the same crate.

In his new home Johnny was kept on a screened porch for several days, then allowed to fly free. When school began, Jim and Stuart took the bus each day. At first Johnny did not seem

*Queenie the dog was jealous of Johnny the crow when Johnny first joined the family. Later they became good friends and traveled together in the same pen from Chicago to Florida.*

to notice. Then one morning when Mrs. Anderson walked with her sons to the bus stop, Johnny rode on her shoulder. He saw the yellow bus depart with his two friends inside. Suddenly he sprang into the air and flew to the top of a nearby tree. He stared after the bus until it disappeared. Then, as Mrs. Anderson watched, Johnny began to fly in constantly widening circles, until he too disappeared.

Probably Johnny spotted the bus parked in the schoolyard. Anyway, he was soon pecking on the window.

For the next several months Johnny went to school almost

every day. Often he flew alongside the bus, then rode the shoulder of one of the children into the school.

Like all corvines, Johnny liked to steal and hide bright objects. And he liked to visit. He would fly from house to house, dropping out of the sky to perch on a porch table or chair. Soon everybody on the island knew Johnny.

Johnny's friendliness may have been his undoing. One day a lady, a temporary visitor to the island, came to the Anderson home. She wanted to buy Johnny for her son, and offered $300. It was a huge sum, but Jim and Stuart only shook their heads. Johnny was a member of the family. They couldn't sell Johnny.

Next day the lady left the island, going back north. At exactly that same time Johnny disappeared. Every child on the island joined in the search for Johnny. Perhaps he had been killed by an owl or raccoon or cat. But not even a feather was ever found.

Everyone felt sure that Johnny had been crow-napped.

*All crows love to play tricks, but only a pet would have the confidence to try this.*

All corvines have tremendous appetites. They not only eat almost anything, but lots of it. A naturalist in South Africa who had two pet ravens found that each one would eat almost half its body weight each day. This is about the same as a one-hundred-pound boy eating forty-five pounds of food a day. If the ravens were given so much food they could not eat it all at once, they carefully hid it. Once the male raven, named Roko, decided to hide some leftover meat underneath an open door. Carefully Roko poked the meat under the door, then put a leaf in front to make sure it could not be seen. Still uncertain, he walked around the door to look from the other side. And, sure enough, the meat was showing. Now he poked the meat back under the door but, still unsatisfied, he went back to the first side to look again. And once more the meat was showing. Once more he shoved the meat under the door and replaced the leaf to hide it. Once more he walked around to the other side to make sure.

This time, in obvious disgust, Roko picked up the meat and flew off to hide it elsewhere.

All corvines have a pouch in the throat in which they can store food—or almost anything else—and then bring it back up at will. This is why a crow may seem to eat a piece of meat, or swallow a brightly colored marble, and then have it again a few minutes later. Dr. John Watson, an American ornithologist, was doing some house painting when he saw to his horror that Edgar Allen, his pet crow, seemed to be bleeding to death. At least its bill and half its head were bright red and dripping what appeared to be blood. On closer inspection, it turned out to be the red paint Watson was using on his house.

Watson never knew if the crow had actually drunk some paint, held it in its pouch, or merely dipped its head in out of curiosity. And except for its strange look, the bird suffered no ill effects.

*The mailbox marked the end of Dr. Watson's property, and the limit of adventures. His pet crow would not go beyond this point.*

This crow had one trait that Dr. Watson never quite understood. If Watson was riding a horse around his farm, Edgar Allen might light on his shoulder and ride with him. If he drove his car the crow might fly alongside, or even ride on top. But when he reached a certain point, the crow would go no farther. Instead, it flew back to the house.

And the point beyond which the crow would not go was the boundary line of Watson's property. There was nothing to mark this line, but Edgar Allen would never go beyond it.

79

# 11

# Corvine Species

As mentioned in Chapter 5, some ornithologists divide *Corvus brachyrhynchos*, usually called the common crow, into four subspecies. *Corvus brachyrhynchos brachyrhynchos*, the eastern crow, is slightly bigger than the others and has the widest range. Although called the eastern crow, it can be found throughout most of the United States, Canada, and parts of Mexico. In fact, it breeds as far north as Alaska and as far south as southern Florida, Texas, and Mexico. It is by all odds the most common and widely spread of the crows.

The southern crow (*Corvus brachyrhynchos paulus*) is slightly smaller than the eastern crow and has a more slender bill. Its range is from South Carolina to Texas and sometimes as far north as southern Illinois.

The Florida crow (*Corvus brachyrhynchos pascuus*) is said to be found nowhere except in Florida and is comparatively rare even there. In size it is between that of the eastern crow and the southern crow, but it has large feet for its size.

The western crow (*Corvus brachyrhynchos hesperis*) is smaller than either the eastern or Florida crow, about the same as the southern crow but with a slightly longer wing. It ranges across western North America from British Columbia in Canada to southern California and New Mexico.

*An adult fish crow. Fish crows live chiefly along the beaches of the southern states. This picture was taken at Bulls Island, South Carolina.*

As its name implies, the fish crow (*Corvus ossifragus*) lives close to water. In the United States it may be found along the entire Gulf Coast and along part of the Atlantic Coast, sometimes as far north as Massachusetts. Occasionally it moves inland along large rivers or lakes. It is a comparatively small crow, about fifteen inches in length, some two inches less than most *Corvus brachyrhynchos*, and its voice is not quite so loud. On the other hand it is even more hoarse, often sounding as if the bird had a sore throat.

Fish crows usually nest in small colonies, three or four families fairly close together. They also roost together, but never in the huge numbers in which *Corvus brachyrhynchos* sometimes gather. Instead, a half dozen or so fish crows may roost in one clump of trees, another group in trees a half mile away.

*A rare albino crow*

The northwestern crow (*Corvus caurinus*), like his fish crow relative, lives close to water. In fact, the chief difference between them is that while the fish crow lives along the Atlantic and Gulf coasts, the northwestern crow lives along the Pacific from the state of Washington north to Alaska. Since tall trees are rare in much of its range, the northwestern crow often nests in low bushes or even on the ground. It may also use the same nest for year after year, but not always. These crows gather around Indian or Eskimo villages to feed on any scraps they may find, and since they are rarely troubled, they may become much tamer and less cautious than most crows.

RAVENS

Like their close relatives, the crows, ravens are divided into several species and subspecies. Of these only two species are found in North America: the white-necked raven (*Corvus cryptoleucus*) and the common raven (*Corvus corax*). *Corvus corax* is sometimes separated into two subspecies, *Corvus corax principalis*, the northern raven, and *Corvus corax sinuatus*, the American raven. The difference is chiefly in their range and most persons will settle for calling them all *Corvus corax*, the common raven.

These ravens are found throughout practically all of Canada, from the Atlantic to the Pacific. Along the Pacific they range from the top of Alaska south to Central America. *Corvus corax* is also common in Great Britain and most of Europe. But in the United States, this raven is rarely found east of the Rocky Mountains—with one strange exception: high in the Appalachian Mountains of Virginia and Pennsylvania. Here the birds seldom go lower than 3,000 feet. And here, as well as along mountainous sections of the Pacific Coast, ravens are as apt to nest on the side of a cliff as in the top of a tree.

The raven is bigger and stronger than the crow, about twenty-one inches in length compared to the common crow's seventeen inches. Also, its head and bill are heavier. Otherwise almost everything you can say about the crow is also true of the raven. In the far north, a dead whale may feed a whole flock of ravens

*In mountains, the raven often builds its nest on the side of a cliff*

*These ravens on the Mohave Desert in California had no tree in which to nest, so they have used a large cactus.*

for a winter—with crows joining in. Ravens feed along the edge of ice floes looking for dead seals. They steal and eat the bait from fox traps and have been known to kill and eat a trapped fox. In the summer, like crows, they feast on the eggs of seabirds and in the autumn stuff themselves on berries.

Man is just about the only major enemy of ravens, and where men do not molest them they become very tame. One naturalist wrote that ravens, feeding on scraps around Indian villages in northern Canada, were never troubled by the Indians. The ravens, he said, "were as tame as chickens." But where hunted and killed the raven quickly becomes as shy and cautious as any crow.

Crows sometimes mob a raven almost as frantically as they mob the great horned owl. The raven, however, doesn't seem too troubled by such attacks. Faster on the wing, the raven may simply outfly the cawing crows. Or it may let one come close, then whirl out of reach. Far from being in danger, the raven often seems to be playing a game, letting one crow after another come close, then dodging.

The raven's voice is much like that of the crow, with a wide variety of calls. And taken young, it, like the crow, will make an excellent pet.

THE WHITE-NECKED RAVEN

From its name it would seem that the white-necked raven (*Corvus cryptoleucus*) is the one American corvine that can be quickly and easily told from all its inkblack relatives. Indeed, the feathers about the neck and upper breast are half white, half black. Unfortunately only the inner half, closest to the body, is white. Usually the white is not visible unless a strong wind ruffles the feathers or the bird's head is bent far over to pick up food. Although the white-necked raven is perhaps a half inch bigger than the common crow, it is very difficult, most of the time, to tell them apart.

This is not true, however, during the mating season. Describing this, one naturalist wrote: "During early April the raven begins to engage in his courtship . . . It is then the community takes to the sky, and the male especially is wont to perform in the air—soaring, side-slipping, wheeling, and tumbling . . . At this time his snowy-lined neck-piece becomes so enlarged that the feathers stand straight out like a fluffy boa, while those on his chin upturn at an acute angle." At such times it is easy indeed to identify the white-necked raven.

*Corvus cryptoleucus* is chiefly a bird of the western deserts

*The beautiful green jay doesn't look like a crow, but it does belong to the family Corvidae.*

and plains. Over a hundred years ago when buffalo roamed the plains and wagon trains were first moving west, the white-necked raven was often seen as far north as Kansas, Nebraska, and Colorado. It fed on the carcasses of dead buffalo and followed the wagon trains to pick up other scraps. But when the buffalo were killed off and iron trains replaced the wagons, the white-necked ravens gradually disappeared from this area. Now it is rarely seen except in western Texas, Arizona, New Mexico, and southward into Mexico.

Since trees of any kind are rare in much of this area, the white-necked raven builds its nest in whatever is available. This is quite likely to be low-growing mesquite trees, or even cactus.

Technically, crows and ravens are not only related to the rooks (*Corvus frugilegus*) and the jackdaws (*Corvus monedula*) of Europe, they are also kin to the various jays and magpies. Altogether these many species make up the scientific family Corvidae. The jays and magpies, however, do not have the same first name of *Corvus*. They don't look like their *Corvus* relatives, and the relationship is too slight for this book to consider.

# 12

## Pearl

When I began this book I had already spent a lot of time watching and studying wild crows. I had met several pet crows that belonged to friends. But I'd never had a crow of my own.

It was too late in the year to find a nest with babies in it, so I phoned Pam Stewart, the "Bird Lady" of Bradenton, Florida. When anyone in this area finds an injured or helpless bird, he takes it to Mrs. Stewart. Around her yard and house wander pelicans, sea gulls, big and little owls, and birds of a dozen other species. I asked if she had a crow.

She did. It was a young crow, not yet a year old. Someone had shot it, and someone else had picked it up and brought it to Mrs. Stewart. By now it was fairly well. But Mrs. Stewart doubted it would ever become a true pet; it had been flying free of its nest when shot.

I named it Pearl, brought it home, and placed it in a big cage with food and water. Then I sat back to watch. Terrified, the bird fluttered back and forth. About the third time across the cage, it flew into a swinging perch and its foot got caught in the bent wire. There it hung upside down.

It took a few moments to get her free. And, as Whitney Dough learned from his pet Andy and the runaway wagon, a crow that has been hurt and frightened will never forget. Pearl

*Pearl liked to bathe, both in the water bowl and in a shower from the hose.*

never quite got over being afraid of me. There was, however, more to it than just the incident of the swing. I never knew who had originally shot and injured her. Probably it was a man. For Pearl was afraid of all men, particularly anyone carrying a stick. If she saw a man working in the yard with a rake or hoe she became frantic. She would fly wildly back and forth across the cage, or hurl herself against the bars.

On the other hand she was never really afraid of my wife, Jeannie. Little by little they became friends. Jeannie would bring Pearl crackers coated with peanut butter—Pearl *loved* peanut butter—and the bird would sidle up to the edge of the cage to eat from her hand. If Jeannie leaned close, Pearl would ruffle her feathers, bend her neck, and make surprisingly soft cooing noises.

But never, even for peanut butter, would she take food from my fingers.

Pearl did not like any sudden change. At first her water was put in an aluminum pan. All right. But then Jeannie bought a dark-colored bowl for the water. The bowl was on the floor of the cage, and Pearl stayed on the highest perch until we thought she'd die of thirst. Finally we took out the dark bowl and lined it with aluminum foil. Pearl dived down, drank, then climbed in to bathe. She then began to peck at the aluminum foil. Bit by bit she tore it up until only the dark bowl remained. And having come on it gradually, through her own action, it no longer troubled her. From that point on she drank happily from the bowl.

It was the same when for the first time we took her cage outside. On the porch the floor of the cage was covered with newspapers. Outside it was put directly on the grass. Pearl sat on her topmost perch and refused to come down until we put papers on the ground. Then she came down, tore up the newspapers, and from that time on happily accepted the grass floor.

My intention from the first was to make Pearl into a true pet, if possible, but one free to come and go if she wished. To do this she must be able to fly better than she could in a cage. So one day, with the cage on the screened-in porch, we opened the cage doors. Pearl backed to the far side of the cage and sat there.

It was the third day before she came out, cautiously, and climbed to the top of the cage. A few hours after that she was flying freely about the porch.

I had expected that with the early dark she would go back into the cage. But Pearl apparently couldn't find her way. Crows are intelligent—at least most crows are—but the cage doors seemed to mystify Pearl. Three nights we had to catch her—at least my wife did; I couldn't get near her—and put her back in her cage. Then, suddenly, the whole situation became clear to her. From that time on Pearl went in and out at will.

All this while we were trying to teach Pearl to talk. I wanted

*Pearl and Jeannie talking crow. Pearl never learned to speak human, but she taught her owners a lot of crow.*

her to say, "Nevermore!" Jeannie tried to teach her to say, "Pretty Pearl." Jeannie would stand by the cage a half hour at a time saying, "Pretty Pearl. Pretty Pearl. Pretty Pearl." Pearl would cock her head to one side and yell, "*Caw-w-w. Caw-w.*" Pearl never did learn any English words, but Jeannie got to where she could talk good crow.

Probably it was Pearl's lusty shouting that attracted the wild crows. Sometimes one or two, sometimes a half dozen would light in the tree just outside, making loud noises.

When we put the cage outdoors there was one particular crow —or so it seemed to us; we could never be certain—that came more often than the others. Sometimes it would light on top of the cage. When it did Pearl sometimes climbed up the cage as close to the free bird as she could, but not always. Sometimes she seemed to make a show of all the food she had available, hopping about with bits of it in her mouth while the free bird watched.

Jeannie and I decided there was a courtship going on, though we could not actually know the sex of either bird.

After some three months it seemed time to give Pearl her chance at freedom. For the first time we opened the cage outdoors.

Pearl came out promptly and climbed on top of the cage. A strong wind was blowing and she had never really been in a wind before. She started to fly and the wind seemed to push her back. She turned and went with it, getting higher. Again she turned, into the wind, and flew back over us, across the nearby canal, and into the top of a tall pine. There she clung desperately to a limb whipping back and forth in the wind.

Jeannie began to call, "Pearl! Pearl!" waving a cracker with peanut butter.

Pearl clung to her limb.

A grackle—it probably had a nearby nest—began to dive-bomb the crow. Nothing of this sort had ever happened to Pearl before. She took wing, the grackle close behind. Suddenly another crow appeared, chasing the grackle. The three birds, one close after the other, flew up the canal and disappeared.

That was three weeks ago. Pearl's cage is still in the yard with food and water inside, the door open. Grackles, doves, sparrows, and cardinals go in and out. But Pearl has never come back. Whenever a crow flies low over the yard Jeannie waves and calls, "Pearl!" Sometimes the bird answers and Jeannie says, "That was Pearl. I know it."

# INDEX